the happy book *for* birthdays

501 happy thoughts

the happy book *for* birthdays

501 happy thoughts

CADER BOOKS

Andrews McMeel Publishing

Kansas City

Design by Charles Kreloff

ISBN: 0-7407-1037-0

Library of Congress Catalog Card Number: 00-100439

the happy
book *for*
birthdays

501 happy thoughts

Introduction

Nothing's more fun to celebrate than a birthday. It's your special day, and it comes once a year, whether you're ready for it or not. This book is a little celebration all its own of just some of the things we love about birthdays: parties, presents, and cake to be sure, but also the things we look forward to, the ways we celebrate, and the ways we use them to mark time.

Most especially, we look at what makes a birthday such a special day—the happy ways you can use the day to reflect, indulge, move forward, look back, anticipate, appreciate, and of course, celebrate.

Wishing you hundreds of happy thoughts today and every year on your special day. Happy Birthday!

taking your time

goofing off

a day like no other

a day off from marathon training

celebrating that you are still able to run a marathon

having a three-hour lunch

becoming eligible for Medicare

becoming legal to vote

getting discounts just because you're older

being excessive

getting a driver's license

being chauffeured around

being thankful for what you have

rejoicing in what is good in your life

doing a charitable act

being kind to others

being giving

reconnecting with family

your family does especially nice things for you

remembering old friends

old friends remember you

making a resolution

doing just nothing—it's okay

watching the sunrise

spending the day gardening

treating yourself to new CDs

buying yourself a new book

living life fully

giving thanks that you're alive

taking a moment for reflection

it's a marking point in the year

finding yourself on the continuum

something to look forward to

making wishes

believing wishes come true

gathering friends

it happens only once a year!

a cause for celebration

an excuse for a party

a reason for someone else to plan
the party

it's the yardstick by which we
measure the other 364 days in a
year

remembering what it was like
when you were a kid

indulging your secret lust for royal
frosting

waking up early because you're excited

blowing off things you don't want to do

phone calls from all over the globe

breakfast in bed

your kids are nice to you

your spouse gets up with the kids

you get to read the paper first

you choose the dinner food

trying a new restaurant

an excuse to open a 1986 Yquem

splurging on a new dress

treating yourself to a special gift

when they are over, you don't have to give them another thought for 364 days

a day you don't have to cook dinner

checking in to a posh hotel

flowers at your office

something to look forward to in spring

something to look forward to in winter

something to look forward to in summer

something to look forward to in fall

something to look forward to whenever you're feeling bad

a terrific launch or deadline for a self-improvement project

pizza decorated to read "HAPPY BIRTHDAY!"

getting older is better than the alternative

seeing friends and family

opening presents

getting new things

singing "Happy Birthday"

going to jazz clubs

getting dressed up

being the center of attention for a change

having a baby-sitter once a year

your spouse wearing an apron and nothing else

an excuse for a massage

a reason to play hooky

a chance to have an actual conversation with your partner

a night of the year to have sex

a reason to break out the bubbly

your partner changes all the diapers

your spouse does the late-night feeding

you don't have to take the garbage out

someone else sorts the recycling

you can go all day without saying a cross word to anyone

you don't have to listen to others' problems

someone else makes the reservations

someone else plans the evening's agenda

a surprise visit from old friends

surprise parties

the grandparents take the kids

a reason to make a joyful noise

a reason to whoop it up

an excuse to wear pajamas all day

an excuse not to go to the gym

a reason to go to the gym

a reason to dance

an opportunity to meet friends of friends

the present of another year with
those you love

getting something you always
wanted

getting something extravagant

getting something you'd never
dare to buy for yourself

phone calls from out of the blue

anything can happen and anything
is possible

an excuse to have a little something extra

an excuse to skip school

an opportunity to treat others to dinner

an excuse not to split the check

checks from grandparents

unexpected windfalls

savings bonds

singing waiters

blowing out candles

a day for feeling on top of the world

a day when you get the first piece of cake

a day to wear your birthday suit

your voice mail is full of messages

your horoscope is first in
the newspaper

surprise delivery of
freshly baked cookies

late-night parties

a reason to dance all
night

singing telegrams

stripping telegrams

office lunches

office parties

surprise e-greetings

a reason to say something
nice about somebody

a reason to be thoughtful

picking out a special gift

a time to enjoy giving
something handmade

Party Things

satin ribbons

Mylar balloons

helium balloons

crepe paper streamers

party favors

goody bags

funny hats

clowns

noisemakers

sparklers

confetti

Pin the Tail on the Donkey

Twister

scavenger hunts

pool parties

sleepover parties

bowling parties

you're a year wiser

you still have more brown hair
than gray

you're no longer under your
parent's thumb

you're aging gracefully

you're none the worse for wear

you're getting older and better

you can still wear your college jeans

you've survived a year's worth of change, with a smile

a special dinner, and your spouse cleans the kitchen

a reason for romance

a good time to pop the question

midnight breakfast in your pajamas

a kiss at the stroke of midnight

pulling out old photos

rereading old letters

celebrating how young you feel

a moment to be grateful for good health

you're never too old for fun

Disney World is more fun at fifty than at five

celebrating life

remembering the past

charting the future

reflecting on your successes

enjoying others

finding good in yourself

treating yourself like a king or a queen

eating only the frosting

having whichever buttercream rose you want

for he's/she's a jolly good fellow

"Happy Birthday"—Stevie Wonder style

telling your age . . . or not

a day for your loved one to plan

gift bags

the smell of a birthday bouquet

new lingerie

silk pajamas

silk boxers

roses

taking yourself to the movies

seeing *Gone With the Wind* for the
tenth time

crudités

people jumping out of a cake

a gorilla with a bouquet and balloons

Godiva chocolate

Serendipity frozen hot chocolate

trinkets

tchotchkes

potpourri

bath salts

bubble baths

Chinese food eaten in the bathtub

a long soak with a book

a sensual soak with a lover

a bath, for once, without the kids

sleeping late

staying up all night

watching the sunset

a lazy nap in the hammock

someone else cuts the grass

you get to choose the music; no Barney allowed

a new tie

a celebratory shoeshine

an afternoon dalliance

a lunchtime walk in the park

a date with your dad

a lunch with your mom

a reprieve from homework

dim sum for breakfast

a rose on your pillow

flower petals on your sheets

a gift certificate to a full day at
the spa

a birthday puppy

a birthday kitten

a package from overseas

wrapping paper with balloons on it

lobster dinner

candlelit dinners

a meaningful card

a thoughtful gesture

Indian food—you choose how spicy

celebrating victories

putting defeats in perspective

reflecting on those in your life

a time to tango

savoring a wine you've been saving

embarking on the future

keeping a promise to yourself, or to someone else

friends singing off-key

extra mail

extra e-mail

birthday spankings

choruses of "How old are you now?"

a charitable donation in your
name

party horns

swing dancing

jitterbugging

waltzing

limbo!

birthday drinks

a reminder to keep growing
emotionally and spiritually

resolving to learn more

celebrating what you've achieved

assessing what's left to do

dwelling on your hopes for your
children

dreaming dreams for yourself

Birthday Cards

sappy cards from your parents

dirty cards

cards with music chips

cards that spill confetti all
over your lap

special cards from your kids

a card from your lover that
touches your heart

silly cards

remembering what is important to you

stopping and being thankful for reaching this day

fresh-squeezed juice

timely toasts

good-natured ribbing

thank-you notes

hugs

a perfect gift

a thoughtful note

a family party

a birthday banner

a present made by a child

the sweet, smoky smell of blown-out candles

a shopping spree that someone else finances

patent leather party shoes

boys in blue blazers

disposable cameras

posing for pictures

candid shots

flashes going off

leaving generous tips

saving a piece of cake for
someone unable to attend

counting the year's blessings

remembering a really great year

a day for luxury

a day for simplicity

pizza parties

skating parties

a birthday barbecue

trick candles that won't blow out

a birthday crown

party hats

a magician with a rabbit

guest books

a beach picnic

taking up golf

taking up tennis

taking up hiking

finding shapes in the clouds

watching for shooting stars

making a new friend

volunteering at a hospital

volunteering at a homeless shelter

taking a break from your kids

remembering who you are

cleaning out your closets, physical
and mental

breathing deeply

a day to exhale

taking in everything with fresh
eyes

renewing your vision

weeding out the old

planting a new garden

visiting someone elderly

a day to bloom in the garden in
which you are planted

using your time well

shooting the breeze

taking up fishing

playing miniature golf

riding a carousel

melting cotton candy on your tongue

having your fortune told

gazing into your bright future

smelling bread baking

cuddling your baby several extra times

letting a kiss linger

letting the last note of music hang in the air

letting others tell you what is on their minds

sitting quietly and listening to the music of your life

an opportunity to grow

an opportunity to focus

a moment to share with someone you love

Well-Wrapped Presents

exquisite wrapping

velvet bows

happy-face wrapping paper

wrapping paper with dalmatians on it

tissue paper

unexpected presents

presents from secret admirers

homemade presents from your kids

gag gifts

presents inside of presents inside of presents

French wire ribbon

gift boxes

a moment to reflect on loves past

remembering those who have shaped your life

thanking a mentor

mending fences

repairing a relationship with a friend

letting someone know you wish they would be in your life more

making up with your sister or brother

balancing your checkbook

getting your résumé together

being thankful for a great boss

thanking someone for making the past year special

clarifying your hopes for the year ahead

dreaming about having a baby

Sweet Sixteen parties

fortieth birthday dinners

seventy-fifth birthday bashes

a day passed in quiet reflection

giving something back

returning a favor

making time for your partner

reading an extra bedtime story

traveling far away

staying close to home

sharing an ice cream soda

going back to the old neighborhood

calling your old college roommate

being glad for the roads you have traveled

reflecting on a road not taken and determining if you care to rechart your course

reminiscing with abandon

putting a difficult past behind you

opening new doors

forgiving your parents

thanking parents for a job well done

skipping down the street

smiling at passersby

singing in the shower

singing in the car as you go to work or take the kids to school

doing a jigsaw puzzle

reading the morning funnies

stopping for a cup of tea

Sweet Treats

homemade cake

chocolate cake

hot fudge sundae

crème brûlée

boxed chocolates

chocolate mousse cake

carrot cake

angel food cake

pancakes for breakfast

sponge cake

layer cake

eating cake without guilt

ice cream cake

licking frosting off candles

curling up in an afghan

running with your dog in the park

planting a flower that will bloom
each year around your birthday

treating your child to a banana split

starting an IRA

adding to your savings account

a day to plant a tree

resolving to recycle

scheduling an annual physical

booking a mammogram

slowing things down

turning off the television and
talking to your partner

taking up a new hobby

getting a new bike

walking more each day

initiating a weight-training
program

beginning to prevent osteoporosis

addressing a problem

resolving unfinished business

a moment for company

a moment for long-needed
solitude

making a fresh start

letting things slide

seizing the day

rekindling a flame

tripping the light fantastic

observing and taking in

listening to a favorite piece of
music

eating a favorite food

visiting a beloved relative

reconnecting with a long-lost friend

initiating a home renovation project

starting yoga

adopting a pet

celebrating patience gained

celebrating wisdom earned

starting a heart-smart diet

pigging out

going in-line skating

going skydiving

bungee jumping

going parasailing

skipping shaving

shaving off a beard

letting your hair down

getting a haircut

getting a makeover

listening to cicadas

watching children playing

watching a tadpole change into a frog

watching a butterfly emerge from a chrysalis

listening to the chirping of birds

watching a hummingbird drink
from a trumpet flower

ignoring your wrinkles

deciding on cosmetic surgery

coloring your hair

resolving to return to your natural
color

going sledding

drinking hot chocolate by a fire

laughing with childlike wonder

blowing bubbles

gathering wild flowers

hiking a nature trail

bird-watching

watching old movies until dawn

meeting someone for breakfast

having waffles for dinner

a time for anticipation

a time for merriment and mirth

a time for giddy conversation

a time to throw caution to the wind

convulsing with laughter

abandoning yourself to silliness

going to a museum on your lunch break

not going back to work after lunch

watching *Gilligan's Island* reruns

remembering when . . .

slipping on your wedding dress, just because you can

going to the ballet and dreaming

writing your name with seashells
in the sand

building sand castles, and
watching them wash away

walking on sandbars at low tide

cross-country skiing under a full
moon

chasing seagulls

throwing coins into a fountain

playing the lottery

celebrating beating the odds

being thankful for smart doctors
and skilled surgeons

taking the old buggy out for a spin

driving in a convertible with the
top down

buying yourself a bag of candy

sharing jelly beans with small friends

teaching something you've learned

learning from your students

telling someone you love her

a day to receive love in return

a reason not to step on the scale

a day to wear perfume

a reason to wear something
brightly colored

buying yourself a bouquet

jumping for joy

remembering the essentials:
health, love, life